悟り

SATORI

One American's path to an awareness
of love—through haiku

By

Fletcher H. Maffett

First printing, July, 2025
ISBN: 979-8-218-73976-8

FMB+D PRESS

Preface

I first discovered the word **Satori** in an article in *The New Yorker*. I thought it sounded Italian—or maybe Spanish. I wasn't sure, so I looked it up. It turned out to be Japanese, meaning *"sudden enlightenment."* It was perfect.

I didn't know it at the time, but I tucked that word away for future use—not realizing it would someday become the title of a book. **This book**. A collection of my awkward attempts at writing haiku. Some corny. Some not. All mine. And now, yours.

I became fascinated with writing haiku as a way to understand love in ways I couldn't express aloud. Sometimes it was my way of figuring out if I was in love. Sometimes it was just a goofy attempt to make sense of my feelings.

Over the years—and through a few intimate relationships—haiku became a kind of journaling for me. At first, scribbled on scraps of paper stuffed in a pocket. Later, hundreds stored in my iPhone. What follows are the ones I wanted to share.

Originally, I wanted a full page just for a dedication. But if you've received any of these before—if you've been part of these moments in any way—then this book is dedicated to you. Thank you for making it possible for me to share my own awareness journey.

You know who you are.

your every freckle
a constellation of stars—
i gaze upon you.

☆

you, at my doorstep—
unexpected visitor.
welcome inside me

sometimes haiku waits
to deliver a message—
of bountiful love

i think up haiku...
then i apply it to you.
the words escape me!

(5.7.5)

my heart is a drum
it beats, and beats, and beats, and...
my heart beats for you!

outside our window,
snow piling up on glass panes,
hides the warmth inside.

❄

the thought of your lips,
the taste of your tongue on mine—
sweet summer cherries

you said you love me,
i never saw that coming.
unexpected gift!

sometimes, words just fail
to express the way i feel.
listen to my heart

spring azaleas,
so vibrant, and so alive—
like pictures of you

love, i long for you…
our bodies curled together—
and the moon approves!

☾✦

no compass. no map.
using the stars to guide us—
leading us forward.

each conversation—
character compositions,
hearts and souls revealed

my heart in your hands—
do with it what you see fit.
after all, it is yours

she smiles with her eyes—
her ears, her shoulders, and feet.
so much happiness!

you have touched my heart—
indelible is the print
you leave upon it

my love, i sit here
wondering where you are.
you reveal a glimpse

should i continue
to pursue after your heart?
i'm going with, "yes."

paint on our canvas.
you cannot say we're not art—
untethered colors

🎨

wet and grey outside...
yet the very thought of you
makes my world sunny

if life's a journey
i want you up front with me—
we'll share the driving!

the way i see you—
the strongest woman i know
still melts like butter

○

your radiant eyes
illuminating the night
leads my soul to port

*i have never loved
anyone as much as you
can you give it back?*

🫴

your moon and my sun
mix together in the sky—
blue, purple, orange!

all my poetry
is not lost on you, my love,
if it finds your heart

your greatest weakness,
your vulnerabilities...
i keep them sacred.

the moon in twilight—
a sliver of white in blue,
yet i think of you

you discovered me,
bringing your fruit to my land—
generous bounty!

haiku is painful.
it rips so much from the heart
just to make a point!

to be who i am,
to be worthy of your love,
to be in heaven

☁

each second becomes
an hour—without you near,
like time standing still.

to know someone well
takes more than a thousand nights—
all of mine are yours

📅 17

you deserve much more
than the love you've never known—
look deep inside you

mercurial girl—
slips in and out of herself,
like changing seasons

your heart is so huge—
like the state of nevada,
i'm small within it.

lingering moments—
pictures of you in my mind.
still, i smell your scent.

what typeface to use?
helvetica? bodoni?
illicit affair!

LoVe

to sleep next to you,
take in your warm breath at night,
fills my lungs with you

i believe in you
you have shown me something new,
possibilities!

you, holding my hand—
wondering how i deserve
to have such fortune

when you cheat, you steal.
your lies took so much from us,
it was high stakes theft.

💔

i want to know you
even more than i do now
just to fall deeper

sometimes, i wonder
how you became part of me
without me knowing

my heart is a tune—
until you come close to me
then it's symphonic

no need for poems—
your touch on my shoulder speaks
all the words i need

you've let me inside—
and now your pain has a place
to finally rest

i can't help but think,
how rare it is in this life—
feeling understood

360°↻

the way you look back—
as though you already know
i'm falling for you

☆

this world can be cruel
but i'll always choose to love
whom the others left

you've kissed me deeply
pulling me in completely
deeply inside you!

our syncopation—
not always a steady beat
but we make it dance

🔊

i long to be yours
in the smallest kind of ways:
your hand, in my hand

to lay next to you
immersed with you as you sleep
you fill my senses

so many hours spent
conversations without end
continuous tune

at times, i see you
and i'm reminded of dawn,
taken by the light

☼

you say you love me—
and in the way you hold me,
i know that you do

making love with you
your eyes, seeing into mine—
a candle glimmers

the whole universe
seems centered and aligned
with your love in it

this is what i want,
to be your one and only—
together as one?

⦿

anvil on my heart
lifted by the sight of you
and your sweet kisses

i have never felt
such a stronger sense of love...
i've done something right!

❁

fuck! where is my heart?
i thought i had misplaced it—
but you were holding it

like distant circles,
we have been pulled together
to define new shapes

it occurs to me—
every song ever written
was written for you

📻

a strong heart indeed
is one that can stand the beat
of being beaten

each word that we share—
like candles down a hallway—
our path is so clear

൭ꝺ

you have brought color,
magic, singing, and loving
back into my heart

when you're not near me
i feel like an astronaut—
lost among the stars

my hurricane heart
strewn about and conflicted
and still, you calm it

you didn't break me—
you opened up a locked door,
which provided light!

i will not rush you—
even the stars take their time
to fall within reach.

☆

waking up with you,
swirling ocean of blonde hair
sweeps me out to sea

you said, "i love you."
an unexpected surprise—
i've always loved you!

all i know is this—
despite your walls, i want you.
the climb is worth it

🧱

your laugh, your whisper—
each lingers like a secret
known only to me

🎁

exploring our worlds
as we do with our bodies...
i sail inside you

rock, paper, scissors
no matter what the outcome,
you still always win!

don't lose your sparkle!
within you lives a great light,
you just don't see it.

i want to be there
when your fears take over you—
to shield you from them.

when you look at me
i see the light within you—
warms me like the sun

☀

minutes on the phone
bring me closer to your world—
i start to feel you

please, just understand
i want to be the best thing
you have ever done

🏆

you've shared things with me—
your vulnerabilities,
dark, like a peacoat.

you've let me inside—
i don't see only your heart
you've shown me your soul!

⚡

the touch of your skin—
i lose sight of my senses,
it shutters my world

your first kiss shocked me.
it was when we were talking—
sweet interruption!

the sound of your voice
frequency—gravity
your touch pulls me in

your light is my day—
i see ahead, weeks and years.
our nights are my life.

⏳🕐

too often, the words...
i cannot articulate,
they become haiku!

i'm complicated
and yet, uncomplicated—
strange contradiction!

such scathing review!
we saw how they looked at us.
who were they to judge?

⚖

we turned the corner
and right there—in front of us,
perfect blood red moon!

this is where i find
all the drama that i need—
right here, in haiku.

you, me, and bucket,
watching for meteorites—
quiet fireworks.

☆

we have not always
seen eye to eye on some things,
yet—our hearts agree!

my final haiku
will be written as i die.
and it will be yours.

About the Author

Fletcher Maffett is a designer, storyteller, and lifelong observer of people, places, and moments. He's spent his career shaping brands and visuals—but *Satori* marks the first time he's turned design toward words."

Raised in a military family, Fletcher has lived in more places than he can count, shaped by the cities he's passed through and the people he's held close. These experiences—and a quiet search for connection—fuel both his work and his writing.

Satori is his first book. It began as a personal attempt to say the things he couldn't speak aloud. These haiku are fragments of that journey.

He's still figuring it all out—one haiku at a time.

Building your own haiku

Writing haiku is both fun and challenging. If you've never tried it before, the structure is simple—but strict: three lines, with five syllables in the first, seven in the second, and five again in the third.

- I often use the first line to set up the premise—what I saw, where I was, what I felt.

- The second line builds on that—what impression it left, or how it affected my senses.

- These two lines connect to form a complete thought or observation.

- The third line is the payoff. It's the resounding conclusion—the punch, the hug, the kiss.

It's the thing that lingers.

If you're curious about other haiku voices, check out the Japanese masters—Bashō, Buson, and Issa—or even Michael Stipe of R.E.M. fame. Artists are everywhere. You just have to notice them.

COLOPHON:

This book was set entirely in the Minion Pro typeface family. The background patterns are derived from traditional Japanese textile and paper designs.

The icons throughout were created to reflect how I felt in each moment—my interpretation of the situation, emotional or otherwise.

Some may be obvious. Others not so much.

My apologies if any were stumpers.

I guess you had to be there.

www.ingramcontent.com/pod-product-compliance
Lightning Source LLC
Chambersburg PA
CBHW051431090426
42737CB00014B/2922

* 9 7 9 8 2 1 8 7 3 9 7 6 8 *